REASONS
FOR GOING TO
CHURCH

50
REASONS
FOR GOING TO CHURCH

Revised Edition

T. N. Earl

THE *Alpha* PRESS

BRIGHTON • CHICAGO • TORONTO

2 4 6 8 10 9 7 5 3 1

First published 1987 by Arthur H. Stockwell Ltd.
Revised edition published 2016 in Great Britain by
THE ALPHA PRESS
PO Box 139   Eastbourne BN24 9BP

British Library Cataloguing in Publication Data
A CIP catalogue record for this book is available from the British Library.

Paperback ISBN 978-1-898595-69-4

Typeset & designed by The Alpha Press, Brighton & Eastbourne.
Printed by TJ International, Padstow, Cornwall.

Contents

Preface to the First Edition

Church attendance in the United Kingdom has dropped dramatically in numbers since the end of the Second World War and no longer can the country be called Christian. To many people, moral values are no longer of prime importance and the incidence of crime has reached new heights; while violence has plumbed sickening depths of depravity. In the media, as in life, profanity abounds.

In this situation church-going, law-abiding people, whether committed Christians or not, tend to live closer together for reassurance and safety. They depend more on the Church and each other, and less on the outside secular world.

Some small Christian sects and denominations have always believed in a doctrine of non-participation in worldly matters; for example, not exercising their voting franchise, shunning politics and even local councils, refraining from many secular activities such as watching TV or visiting places of entertainment.

While this way of living the Christian life is under-standable and can always be justified, turning your back on society because you do not like the look of it or are even frightened by it, is in itself no solution to the problem of living in a very dangerous world.

Most of the clergy know this, and that is why they are often seen in the wrong light when they openly and publicly proceed at times to redress the balance in some way by liberalising some aspects of theology and doctrine.

This book is a simple attempt to reiterate the truth that man being in a sense naturally religious would like 'to go to a Church' no matter what form of building or institution that may be: put another way, worship given the right conditions is not foreign to man.

People's reasons and perhaps excuses for devotion and worship in Church are diverse, sometimes simple and at times complicated; and if the non-attenders knew that many of the regular church-goers were not part of a 'saved' elite withdrawing from the real world, but ordinary social animals like themselves with the same basic nature, who would admit to one or many of the reasons given in this book, then perhaps such a realization might encourage them to return to a place of worship again or to attend for the first time. That is the purpose of this book.

It is entitled '50 Reasons' because the reader will find at least on average two reasons in each of the twenty-five sections. Parts of what is written may not find favour with some of the clergy, but I didn't set out to say something pleasing to them. This book is for ordinary people. It seems to me that neither the narrow doctrine of the fundamentalists, nor the liberal theology of the established Churches, producing respectively an exclusive club and a semi-secular theatre, will solve the problem of non-attendance.

If you as an individual feel like going to Church, no matter for what reason or cause, then go! – as long as you can justify it to yourself, because in reality that is what everyone else does anyway.

With no knowledge of Greek or Hebrew, the author, not a student of Theology doesn't presume to have any sophisticated scholarly knowledge of the Bible, but is convinced that the Gospel and the message from God is not one of waiting for Him to do things, but waiting *on* Him by worship and prayer so that *we* may do things.

The contents have been influenced by twentieth century theology, but more so by observation of the laity and human affairs. We should underpin the decency and goodness of the vast majority of ordinary people who might refrain from going to Church because they see God prescribed there, all parcelled up and labelled. If you like the label and abide by the rules and follow the leader, that's fine. But if you do not wish to surrender your independence, you are then reluctant to go to Church regularly, if at all.

This book says that you can go to Church without conforming to or surrendering to anyone.

Many people are doing just that and are happy and satisfied doing so – their lives spiritually and other-wise, immeasurably richer.

Preface to the Second Revised Edition

A revised edition requires this preface since many changes both in life and in the World have evolved with the passage of time.

There are amendments and additions to the original text, but with little change to the meaning or the emphasis on ethics.

The progress of Science is limitless in this digital, electronic age, leading to especially, easy access to the Internet with intrusion of private lives.

We now have inter alia, political correctness, compensation culture, extreme self-indulgence, celebrity gratification and the social media.

However the human requirements; physical, mental and spiritual remain paramount.

In philosophy there always will be logic and metaphysics and the works of the great Thinkers and in religion there are Theology, Dogma, Doctrine and Ethics.

Some would argue that Science and Religion are getting closer to each other; that the atheist's belief in the Quantum Physics "theory of a parallel Universe" has resonance with the Christian's belief in pursuit of the Holy Spirit.

Generally people seek security, in and acceptance of, their own faith and beliefs.

Much herein can be said to be ecumenical in its original derivative sense and so in no way is it meant to be disrespectful to people of other faiths who may go to Synagogues, Mosques or Temples.

The emphasis, if any, is on ethics as the "scenarios" or "cameos" are simple representations of human nature and not dogmatic theological assertions, for the obligation to go to Church on the part of committed Christians and those who believe in God.

1

Nature's Reasons

Martin Deakin, although appearing to be deeply engrossed in the sermon, was in fact preoccupied with the state of a ewe he had to leave earlier and hurriedly in order to get to Church on time. Farming all his life, he had hardly ever missed attending Sunday worship, but there were many times when it was a hectic, even frenzied, two-mile dash from his house to the House of God.

It had been a busy week between ploughing and lambing, with a few late nights and very early mornings. He never liked losing a lamb so was always in attendance and alert with regard to the ewes. He had had extra work already these last few days because of rejection, and subsequent bottle feed and nursing. One anxious thought set off another. Was he going to have enough silage for his wintered beef, as the wet weather was forecast to continue without any sign of abatement? The late spring this year was going to be a disaster too with regard to future arable yield. At times, not often, he would think of all the tasks that lay ahead. Looking at the preacher, Martin addressed his thoughts to him. If *he* ever had to do it, he would find it daunting to say the least – all the spraying of crops, sheep-dipping, shearing, marketing of livestock, weed destruction before they had time to flower and seed, fencing and drainage, and the harvesting of potatoes and cereals.

Quite a few tasks had to be done every morning, and Sunday was no exception; not only did much depend on the time of year, but also what stock was kept and the type of business generally. He had never at any time questioned why he should go to Church. Religion was in his blood just as much as farming. Perhaps religion was so much a part of him because of farming.

Civilisation and society in Bible times were agrarian, and the books of both the Old and New Testaments were filled with people, stories and parables connected with the land.

Martin Deakin found no difficulty in relating to these historical events and episodes because of his farming life. He understood. For him there was meaning in them. When you live on the land and have to make your livelihood by farming, it is more than just dwelling in the countryside. It becomes an attitude of mind. Your friends are farmers, your relatives are farmers and even your clergyman in the country church may do a little farming to supplement his stipend, the smallness of which was a problem. Martin Deakin had seen the amalgamation of another congregation into his own, forced and necessitated by both shortage of clergy and lack of finance. The number of families in all rural areas had decreased considerably in his time, brought about not only by farm mechanisation and low labour wages, but also by redundancies. With housing available in the town, labour moved there for jobs and better accommodation. His minister was fortunate in that the Church was well endowed, the rent from lettings of about fifty acres in all going directly to augment his income.

The committee saw to it that the maximum expenses

acceptable to the Inland Revenue were allocated in lieu of salary. It seemed to Martin that the Church and farming were industries that always had problems. Apart from the modern scientific or economic aspects, there remained fundamentally the issue of the weather when you talked about farming; and there was the issue of faith when God was discussed. Martin Deakin had always been conscious that he was dealing with living things. Although the harvesting of crops was still the basic function, the husbanding of livestock was more than just environmental control – it was a purposeful and rewarding job. In farming you learned the law of nature, you knew of the forces outside of yourself, you knew that without a faith survival could be difficult. He thought often, reminding himself, of how on the farm or in the country, you were very close to the origins and basics of life. What a dangerous place too! Apart from accidents with machinery and injuries from animals, there were diseases like ringworm and brucellosis, not to mention viral infections, unidentified, undiagnosed and untreated. Among his neighbours and relatives he counted at least a dozen over the same number of years who had been subject to such trouble of some kind. Only farming made you aware of the uncertainty of life. "All that lives must die," he contemplated, not in a fatalistic sense, but in one of realism tied to a strong faith in God, and a positive determination to meet life head-on knowing that all things work together for good to those that believe.

The service he enjoyed was the Harvest Thanksgiving, when all the hard-worked men and their womenfolk too would show their gratitude to God. The gathering-in of the crops at the end of summer and autumn has always been a time of celebration from time immemorial.

Martin Deakin also appreciated that Sunday was the day when people were relaxed, and after the service he would stand around for a few minutes and exchange words with his farming neighbours. In itself it was a good reason for going to Church.

Martin was thinking that to-day he would be going straight home without any delay, having already warned his wife not to linger. During the lambing season in the past years his wife had often helped him, both with the ewes and lambs.

Her main occupation was looking after the grounds around the house, mainly the garden where she grew a few vegetables. Without her he would have little knowledge or appreciation of trees, shrubs and flowers. For many a year there had been rowans, chestnuts, elms and lilacs which they had inherited when they took possession, but they themselves had planted laburnum and cherry trees. Pity, he thought, how mostly all the blossoms on these trees were over by the middle of July. Any spare time she had, always found her in the garden.

Being a partner in their work, she was also a partner when it came to their Christian belief and service. For this he would always truly thank God; to be able to worship together was indeed a blessing.

Now he changed his train of thought, looked around the congregation and tried to concentrate like them on what was being said by the preacher.

After all, that was one reason why he was at the church.

2

One in a Hundred

Our vicar is great. You just don't know how much I look forward to Sunday – to see and hear him. Of course, it wasn't always like that. I was in the army during many conflicts. What I experienced then, and what I saw, was Christless – I came back determined not to be part of the procreation process. Yes, I married, but remained quite resolute that I wasn't going to bring children into this world. What a world! What people! "Man's inhumanity to man" – I had seen it at first hand and as regards the Church – it had lost its way years, if not centuries, ago.

For a long time I remained in that frame of mind, then a new vicar arrived in the town. I was affiliated to a church – you might say a reluctant adherent. I met the new man in the golf club – and he created an impression with me straight away. He bought me a sherry at the bar after we had been thrown together in a two-ball foursome. He was the only clergyman ever to buy me a drink. He was younger than I, but I suppose you could say there was some kind of interest on my part. He was personable and I could relate to him in a nebulous sort of way. My wife dragged me along to the church one Sunday and it wasn't so bad. The vicar was saying something of interest. A few months later I found out why I had an instinctive infinity with him – he had been a padre for five years to an army regiment. After that my Christianity took off – slowly at first.

But don't think this is purely a personal subjective basis for my present belief and faith. I go to church regularly and enjoy it. I like what the vicar says and how he says it. He is a personal friend, but not only to me and a privileged few. That's just the point. He is completely non-conformist in more ways than one. He is a real Christian and asks everyone to call him by his Christian name, which he says is what all Christians are meant to do to each other. He would quite often dispense with formality in the church to welcome somebody back who had been ill, or to talk to some children.

But, for all his cordiality and affability, his principles were never compromised. When the proposal arose to make submission to the authorities for a full bar licence at the clubhouse, he adamantly opposed the motion and spoke for the negative.

He later told me that every week he had to deal with the results of alcohol addiction. He was also in the Samaritans, but wouldn't reveal anything except to say that some of the callers had problems that would make your hair stand on end. He didn't have to spell it out. There is a world of drugs and sexual abuse.

I wasn't born yesterday and knew of all these depravities which a friend of mine descriptively called 'bastrous'. I saw that during his week the padre wears many a hat, but on Sunday he is himself, and at his best.

The order of service in church is not sacrosanct. Some people I know only attend to hear the sermon – not I – I enjoy every part of it because there is a genuine warmth amongst all of us. I go to church now to find out more about God, and secretly I know I attend because I still need the spiritual support of others who have a stronger faith, to supplement my own.

Our preacher's theology is not tainted with personal prejudice so he doesn't have to justify anything he says. He doesn't speculate on what Jesus would have done in this or that situation; nor does he create fictitious stories by putting words into the mouths of the disciples.

He adheres to the text in the Bible keeping it simple, free from ambiguity. He leaves you with a confident, inspired, reverent feeling.

But it is more than that. There is a continuity about the whole act of worship in praise and prayer of adoration, confession, intercession, petition, aspiration and affirmation, all of which are meaningful.

You may ask, if our vicar had to leave or was no longer there, would I still go to church? Quite definitely yes, but not with the same feeling of great expectation.

He is one in a hundred.

But one day he confided to me "I am fortunate in being appointed to this church where there is harmony amongst the members – no discord ever. I have no committees, vestry or anyone telling me what to preach, to do or what to sing.

Having said that I accept suggestions except the *pulpit* is mine and no one can occupy it without my choosing or approval".

3

Doing What is Right

Jean Dempster slowly washed her breakfast dishes. She had ample time before the Pedens called in their car to take her to St. Michael's. She had long-past thought about how much time she had in every day to do all that she needed or wanted to do. It was ten years since her husband had died, and now, at the age of seventy-five, one of her big events in the week was going to Church.

Her only worry this morning was if the Pedens didn't call. What if they were sick or their car had broken down? They just wouldn't simply forget – would they?

Jean was always a church-goer. Brought up by strict parents to attend worship, she never once questioned the unwritten and unspoken precept. Jean wanted to go – always did. It was the right thing to do. Jean was never philosophical, except to say that if you did what was right, then not much would harm you. That's why she never washed or ironed any of her clothes on a Sunday. She believed in being fair to God. "Give Him his place and He will be more than fair to you!" she had often said. God expected her to go to Church – so she went.

Jean didn't heed much what was said by the preachers – it was more or less a matter of believing in Christ and always doing what was right, and then there was the certainty that the rest of the week would go well. Jean knew if she didn't attend Church she would miss out. She looked back to her youth. Reminiscence came easily, but was nebulous.

She recalled how her mother encouraged her to read and learn the Lord's Prayer, also some Psalms and the Shorter Catechism. She was thankful that such instruction had been given to her because, whenever depressed, she would sing out loud a verse of a Psalm or a hymn. Thankfully, because she had always taken God with her every day, she wasn't often in a despondent mood. Over the years her favourite hymn had changed. Just now it was the verse:

> "O Joy that seekest me through pain,
> I cannot close my heart to thee:
> I trace the rainbow through the rain,
> And feel the promise is not vain,
> That morn shall tearless be."

These wonderful hymns with glorious tunes and the words of Holy Scripture had sustained her all her life.

Now, when she was living alone, if she couldn't recall the words, she would whistle the tune. She found whistling a great comfort. It was company. Whistling a tune that came to mind could summon up many memories.

She always had happy memories of her mother, and was grateful for that. Her mother taught her a lot, always talking to her while she worked in the kitchen, laughing about odd events as they went to the library together. She remembered her mother saying you had to read the "right book" and commit as much to memory as possible, as a preparation for the day when the world might throw something nasty at you.

Her reflections then centred on the day, during the war, when she married her Peter, the young flight sergeant. Heady times when one didn't look too far forward, but rather lived from day to day in faith, grasping thankfully what grace came your way.

He went missing over Burma, but she had his son to live for.

After the war, when Peter's best friend asked her to marry him, she was happy knowing that there would be security. She didn't regret it and lived to love her husband although there was no issue from the marriage. They had both been happy. Strange, she thought, how all the men in her life – including her father, had not lived their expected time. Peter, named after his father, had died of leukaemia in his twenties. Yes, she thought to herself, she had a few harrowing vexing moments, but she tholed them. She never complained, never blamed anyone. Now, in a sudden enlightening way, she quietly smiled when admitting to herself that, at these dark sad moments, she was so shocked and numbed to feel any emotion. She had never learned to expect the vicissitudes of life. There was always the unexpected, but maybe she had an inherited stoicism, or she had a simple faith that could be always expanded.

At the sound of a motor car outside, she was startled from her memories. It was just a passing motorist. She put on her coat and hat, and waited a further ten minutes before the Pedens arrived. Jean had not been too anxious by waiting. How could she be if she was doing what was right!

4

No Doctrine is the Doctrine

I go to our Church very regularly, but if it weren't that our Church is so different from the mainstream faith I would then possibly go only when the mood took me. I have a searching probing mind and on a Sunday I know I shall meet people of like intellect. If I were to criticise the minister's sermon or challenge the Apostle's Creed, I wouldn't be looked on as a leper or branded a heretic.

The Spirit of Christian worship is more important than the exposition of Christian doctrine, and this is not only liberating – it is unifying. You might say we are interdenominational or perhaps non-denominational, unorthodox, de-indoctrinated, less dogmatic but more tolerant.

It all adds up to a friendly lively service. There is a common bond of humility in the worship, because no one present, not even the leader, would ever claim to know the complete truth. The sheer honesty of everyone, devoid of any pretence or humbug in relation to what he or she believes, results in a force of love which by its presence and nature is God-given.

You could say we worship God, not the Bible which at times can hinder as well as help one in the pursuit of truth and righteousness. But in attending Church I am also pursuing strength to meet the problems of the ensuing week – to be able to cope with whatever comes along. I can face the week knowing my God is as good as the next man's, long before convocations of divines re-wrote the gospels and added conditions to please their political masters. There are some aspects of doctrine more apocryphal than the Apocrypha.

I don't get hindered in my attempt to commune with God by being in a doctrinal straight-jacket. The word of God may be infallible, but the many human interpretations of the Biblical text certainly are not.

The Westminster Confession of Faith is an anachronism in this century. Many parts of this treatise are a complete affront to man's intellect and understanding. Who is the bigger hypocrite – the man who has read it and says he abides by it, or the man who hasn't – but still says he subscribes to it?

And what of the common Book of Prayer? Has it not long past served its purpose?

In our Church, orthodoxy is not a test of Christian character. I would go further and say that orthodoxy and many things which stem from it, including some ecclesiastical ordinances, may be actually hindering progress of Christian thought and faith.

The present structures and organisational forms of the Churches may be on their way out, but real Christian faith may be on the way in.

The question is: must religion always be a "religious thing?" and its ethics instilled unwittingly.

Many young people in our Church could answer that any Sunday. By introducing drama, dancing and contemporary music into the Church some of the younger generation are operating new forms of faith; forms possibly at one time called secular. The same applies to young people turning their back on material success and giving of years of their lives to other less privileged peoples. These are tangible and practical axiomatic expressions of faith.

The fundamentalists and those following traditional faiths want to save the world, but on their terms where everyone must conform to their doctrine, theology and ideas of behaviour. There is no place for jeans and long hair in their place of worship.

But I'm gladdened to say that some people worship God in their own way and not based on others' religious interpretations.

It is important to remember that Jesus didn't entrust His gospel to the church leaders of His day; but rather to the most ordinary of people.

Can you understand then how in our Church, freed from man-made doctrine, honest worship to our Creator can be the most exhilarating experience; and, because there is no dogmatism, you can spiritually grow and keep on growing. No mortal knows all the answers, but some would let you think that they do.

Thousands of Church leaders are simply perpetuating religious traditions and rituals, out-dated beliefs and superstitions, which have nothing to do with worshipping God in spirit and in truth.

Honest doubt in our Church is welcomed. Can there be any progress; has there been ever any progress without doubt? Doubt about the shape of the world? Doubt about the nature of the universe? Doubt about the biology of man himself – his atoms, his genes?

Do we know all there is to know about God?

Can anyone really understand the Sermon on the Mount from the Authorised Version without a knowledge of Greek or Aramaic?

I go to my Church because there I meet with like minds. Someone is supposed to have said that there is a Church to suit everyone. I've found mine.

5

'Know That I Am God'

Howard Stewart finished off writing his letter, sitting at the table by the window which overlooked the busy street. Momentarily he reflected on how he enjoyed living where he did – in the centre of things. Some people liked the quietness of the country – others the view and at times the noise of living by the sea – but for him – well, his window was a window on the world and, of course it couldn't be more convenient for the university where he was a lecturer of some years' standing.

It was a Sunday morning and a quarter-after-ten had just chimed on the hall clock. A few cars were appearing on the streets with even fewer people walking. It was February – overcast, bitterly cold with some snow still remaining on the rooftops and gardens.

Howard tentatively folded into three his sheet of paper, carefully adjusting it to suit the long unmatching white envelope the size of which he couldn't even guess at, before pressing down the folds permanently. He liked to take time about things like that – being methodical, he reassured himself, was good for you. He then quickly inserted the letter into the envelope, which when sealed and turned over he addressed in his gently right upward sloping hand. Whatever his shortcomings he held considerable pride in knowing that his handwriting possessed an elegant, distinguished and legible style, seldom found now in the younger generation.

It was time to prepare to go to Church. As his wife was not feeling too well and was staying at home this morning, he had decided to walk and, on the way, drop the letter into the post box. Yes, he thought, he'd better start. There might be the odd chore for his wife, certainly his shoes to polish, his clothes to brush. The service commenced at eleven, and he preferred to be in his seat at least ten minutes before the hour, to have a few moments of reflection when he valued the composure and stillness which enveloped him. Howard knew that some of his acquaintances, and others no doubt, wondered why he should be so regular in the pews when he himself could very well be in the pulpit. Of course, he did preach more than occasionally. He was a Master of Arts in Classics and English Literature of St. Andrew's, and a graduate in Theology at Edinburgh, but he had decided on education and administration rather than pastoral work.

But he did enjoy attending Church because more than once recently he had been helped, and therefore he approached his worship with great expectations. The minister himself was a scholarly type, and that suited him.

People might have been surprised if they had known of his doubts, and yet why should they? A psychiatrist can himself be subject to stress, a builder could easily have problems with a house he built for himself, an accountant could have his own personal finance in a mess – so why should a theologian not have a few irreverent thoughts?

When he was sitting in the pew, quite often he would hear the same words, the same text that he often had delivered himself, but a change of emphasis by the man in the pulpit would cause him to see and accept an additional awareness of forgiveness or toleration.

Having brushed down the lapels, collar and back of his blue coat, he quickly slipped into it, grabbed an umbrella from the stand, had one quick approving look at himself in the mirror and with a "cheerio" to his wife, he stepped outside to face the elements on his march to Church. He had a five-year-old Ford in the garage, but he preferred to walk as often as possible. It was not only good for him, but he enjoyed walking as a recreation and he never knew whom he would meet. While striding out, he could deliberate on many things without having to watch for pedestrians and traffic, as when he himself was behind a wheel.

As he sat in the pew, before the choir had entered and during the organ-playing, he reminded himself again how his friend and colleague had sustained him from the pulpit. He reflected on that sad time in his life. The sort of thing that happens to other people – or perhaps in books or plays or films. A time when his faith was put to the test, and although he came through, he couldn't in all honesty say it hadn't left a scar. As he sat there in his pew, he was still able to retrieve quite easily from his memory the events that led to the period of anxiety – the day his wife told him that his only unmarried daughter was pregnant to the boy she had been friendly with during the last two years of Sunday School and Bible Class.

First he had blamed his wife – then himself – then Christ. Why had He let him down? It was a perplexing time. He tried unsuccessfully not to show disappointment and shock. He hoped not to speak reproachfully. He endeavoured to keep calm but alas became entrapped in the family dialogue. He knew he began thinking about himself; worrying about his own pride rather than the young folk who needed his help at that delicate time.

Slowly with prayer, at first alone then with the others, they struggled through to understanding and love. He and his wife provided security and reassurance. All the theology and learning were, in the end, of little effect. He found that a text in the Bible, or a verse of a hymn, a word from his clerical brother, a firm long-sustained handshake were the outward things that helped him. Strangely he discovered in his daughter and her boyfriend a number of very surprising, but endearing, characteristics he had never dreamed were there. With prayer he surrendered the couple to God's loving care.

One verse from Psalm 46 stood out then, and he had kept it on his lips ever since: "Be still, and know that I am God."

After the initial furore, they were married in Church and went to work and live nearby. Attending worship had greatly helped him then. He was knocked out of his reverie by his colleague announcing the first Psalm to be sung. Yes, once again he was looking forward to another hour-and-a-half of worship which for him meant contemplation, adoration and thanksgiving in prayer and song, affirmation and assurance of his faith.

Nowadays he didn't feel so evangelical as he used to be – leaving that to the younger brethren to pursue. Nowadays he didn't worry too much about predestination as he was getting near the end of his career; knowing that he had some kind of calling from God and leaving it at that. Nowadays he didn't concern himself about the state of Scottish society – undermined by the Irish immigrants and the Highland mythology and romanticism. Perhaps he was becoming a little selfish and introspective, but then when he had his books he was never bored with his own company.

He stretched forth his hand for the hymnal and sat back at peace while he fingered for the correct page.

Then he wondered if the sermon would be as brilliant as last week's. It was on the Lord's Prayer and, with half-an-hour gone, his colleague closed after only reaching "as it is in Heaven".

It is surprising where the best preachers find the best sermons.

6

Public or Private

We were married in Church, but subsequently didn't bother to attend often on Sundays. About two years later, we were at an Evangelical crusade when Mark stood up publicly as a first step in his commitment. I was so surprised at first I can't remember what my initial feelings were, but quickly I knew I had to be with him at that moment. Empathy and love were my intuitive emotions, and I didn't like to see him stand there on his own. Some smart psychologist might say that it was possessiveness that made me stand up too, but that is not true. While the praise of music and prayer proceeded, we walked up to the front and went through the counselling together. Mark became a dedicated publicly-known and accepted Christian, and has attended Church regularly ever since. I go with him always, but a part of my own personality has died. Knowing I have surrendered a part of my own self to Mark, before and after his conversion, which did change his life and has meant so much to him, I haven't told the truth. I suppose he thinks I have made as sincere and deep a commitment as himself. He says it is reassuring to have me beside him.

Church attendance didn't mean much to me before I became married, but to be truthful I find it now helpful in my married life, a type of private insurance in keeping the union loyal. First of all, you are mixing with people whose own marriages are likely to be stable or more stable than average.

With divorce running at one in three, anything to minimise risk of a breakdown in relationships is to be welcomed. I would take divorce as a personal failure; as indicating that there was something wrong in me which helped to bring it about. Of course that is not always the case, but that is what the public would say also.

Secondly, both partners, by attending worship, are accepting the same values together. Thirdly, by giving God his place in your life you are making yourselves, however slightly, just that little less selfish.

Ours is a mixed marriage and nobody, least of all our friends, gave it a chance. The odds of failure are higher and then there are problems of the children's upbringing and education. The Bible says you shouldn't be unequally yoked, but how many today, much to their sorrow, pay scant attention to that.

Many people including friends and relations told us how difficult it would be. How will you educate your children? How will you worship? How will you escape from arguments concerning religion? How will you get on with his side? How will he be able to accept your beliefs? It was how – how – how?

There was no logical answer to any of these questions, but I have found that experience has solved some of them. I'm afraid I didn't keep in step with my family, but then I must have heard a different beat. So far I have been happy, but I know even some of my family cannot forgive me for that achievement. Regrettably, I am blamed for turning my back on my upbringing.

Yes, I made some promises to the priest, but in reneging on these I'm no different from many others.

I'm not married to the chapel or to the priest, whom I found surprisingly sympathetic and understanding. He remains now a friend, and more of an equal.

The clergy's attitude is that any Church is better than no Church.

I feel married to experience. I worship my own God – not even Mark's. In actual fact, I haven't had a great deal of time to think about these things because, on getting married, Mark took the opportunity of buying out the family grocery business, with which he had been since leaving school, and I gave up my job to be in the shop with him. It's been hard, rewarding work. Going to Church on a Sunday is a kind of rest for me, and that is another worthwhile reason. Six days' opening is enough for us and I cannot understand the hue and cry for Sunday opening. Some people have to work on Sunday to keep the wheels of the country turning, and no one will deny the work of necessity and mercy; but to use an overworked phrase, the silent majority do not wish a secular Sunday.

That other laboured phrase, public opinion, is something about which we also have to be circumspect. Public opinion, we are misguidedly informed by media, is what matters – not honesty or truth or people's rights, feelings and privacy. Then the media proceed to contrive by selection this rebellious public opinion to meet their own personal, religious, social and political beliefs; and then to foist this moulded opinion on an unsuspecting public. I find working in the shop and going to Church on Sundays are both places of meeting with ordinary people, people with their feet on the ground.

When you attend worship, what matters is private opinions, private beliefs and private faith. I have a number of reasons for going to Church. They are mine

– they are private – they are important to me and, I trust, in the eyes of God justified.

7

Unfashionable Preaching

My Church is the Cathedral. It is important to me that it is open every day. It means I can visit it when I like, for instance when I feel a desire to get away from the city and the world. It is an escape and I make no apology for that. We are so fortunate because even at the Sunday services we have a Bishop and a Dean and their clerical assistants who talk about God – a God of love and grace. I said it was an escape from the harsh world – the real material world of competition and capital, pleasure and profit, indulgence, violence, poverty, disease, depravity – I could go on ad nauseum.

Yes I can really shut out all that when I attend worship, because our preachers talk about God.

You won't find them leading a crusade for better houses or some disadvantaged group. They seldom mention Iraq or Afghanistan – nor will you hear them talking about apartheid or nuclear disarmament. They do not remind us of this horrendous world, the noise of which we shut out literally when we close the door. It may be unfashionable preaching, but I think that is their success as persons and as preachers, which you may judge any time by joining the ever growing band of worshippers. I am not saying they never pray for Africa's starving millions or never exhort us to do something positive whether it be to confess our sins or give generously to some lost cause.

But by their own piety, assurance and exemplary devotion we can begin to feel and then *know* there is something else – a spiritual dimension.

Our hearts and minds quicken to a divine presence. We are fortunate to have these men as our spiritual leaders. Is that not what we all want at the very least from our Church? Some glimpse of God? The so-called social gospel, which has been popular this century, could really be a distraction, in the sense that it diverted attention from the true Kingdom which is not of this world.

When the fashionable preachers talk about relating to everyday things and making religion meaningful and relevant – they have fallen into the trap of trying to marry the Kingdom with the world. They were not meant to be joined and I believe that people do not attend Church to be reminded of this world; rather they go hopefully to hear about God's world.

It is absolutely reprehensible to find some clergy exploiting the social gospel; in many instances to further their own ambitions, albeit only within the clerical hierarchy.

Anyway, our men talk compellingly about that Someone in that Someplace in that Sometime to which we all secretly and perhaps intuitively aspire. Is that not religion? When I go to Church – the world is shut out for an hour or so, my spirit is lifted and I believe again in eternal values. For a short while, I yearn for grace which I know is my only permanent salvation. God seems a little nearer and He is alive again.

The building and its architecture help very much to this end. That is another very important reason why I worship where I do. Man has always built great temples to God; buildings erected for the sole purpose of worship, although size by itself is not a measure of its importance or spiritual sincerity.

Many have monastic origins of great historical and ecclesiastical interest, but some are newly built in the twentieth century and probably have a more meaningful relationship with the laity.

The Cathedral itself is of a Gothic style and bestows more than dignity and grandeur. It engenders command and importance.

The massive size and height of the columns supporting the galleried cloisters above the nave's buttressed walls leave you in awe as you gaze up and see the light streaming in the clerestory windows. The privacy of the transepts, not seen in their entirety from the nave or chancel, unfolds in the vaulted arches supporting the central tower. The detailed carved dressing of the stonework tells of a time when men knew they were working to the glory of God, as evidenced by the window tracery depicting a special Trinity meaning. The spaciousness and voids between the bare stone just speak God, emphasised by the magnificent finishings to the altar and chancel where the clergy officiate. I never tire of the wonder of it because on taking time I can always discover something new, especially in the rich ornamental symbolism cut in the stone reliefs.

The stained-glass leaded lights comprising mosaics in patterns and figures of religious importance, so diffusing the daylight, not only provide a meaningful addition to the interior, but also soften, enliven and create a conducive atmosphere for piety and devotion.

Here is a place steeped in historical religious majesty for hundreds of years, protecting the faith and beckoning you to worship God. The whole edifice intimidates you into piety, leaving you inspired and spiritually refreshed. There is sanctity.

Such a place puts anyone, on entering, into the right frame of mind for worship, and this perception is not something that quickly disappears on leaving. With the Cathedral open every day, it is not then just a "Sunday only" worship discipline.

What a regal inheritance!

I can't imagine worshipping anywhere else.

8

The Girl from Glendaruel

Amanda walked down the right-hand aisle behind her mother, who followed her father in a processional way, with little Timothy at the rear. At the pew in front of the column which supported the balcony and marked the half-way point between the vestibule door and the communion table her father stopped and allowed his family to file into their seats before taking his place on the outside.

Amanda had just reached her sixteenth birthday with her examinations recently concluded. She had grown and developed early and fully, and nature had bestowed attractive provocative thighs and breasts. This summer, attired in her nylon dresses, she was conscious of having reached womanhood and possessing an allure. The opposite sex was both attractive and challenging. She met a number of boys at the Youth Club, but one in particular took her fancy – Derek McLeod. The trouble was that he didn't always attend the club, but he regularly came to Church.

They lived in a Scottish rural area, their homes far apart. Although she cycled to the shops, for longer distances she was fetched and carried by her mother or father in the family car. She didn't meet people as often as she would have if living in the town, except perhaps in the summer when more outdoor events took place.

She liked living in that part of Argyll especially in summer when it was easier for her to visit her friends and relations on Loch Fyne and Tighnabruaich where she sailed. There it was idyllic and she loved it.

This morning they were early, so Amanda looked around casually and then focussed directly to her left. In this sober, even severe-minded Kirk it was almost a sin to turn your head sideways, but she saw that Derek and his family had not arrived. She felt a mild disappointment. She hadn't seen him since last Sunday when no opportunity to talk to him arose.

She and her family had at the end of the service departed from the church without any loitering to speak to anyone; not to mention the annoying fact that worshippers in her aisle seemed always to exit more quickly than the others. All week she had been thinking of to-day when she hoped to see Derek. Soon she was lost in her secret thoughts. If she had been sent to the same school in Dunoon she would have been able to see Derek every day. But more than that, they would have been involved together in sport and other school societies, such as the dancing club. Now the school dance – that really would be something if she could inveigle him into going to that, but what was the use in hoping for that, when the invitation was a block one sent out by the Head, and nobody knew which boys, if any, would turn up on the night. No, it would have to be the Youth Club outing that held out the best prospect of establishing a good relationship. But what if he thought her too young? This whimsical speculation of possibility would not daunt her as she had time to fulfil this scheme. Why did she come every Sunday to Church – she never asked why – it was expected of an obedient teenage daughter. So it was with Derek, but after this year he might be leaving for university. The outing was not for another month and she must find out, if not to-day then next Sunday or the next one again, if Derek was going. He just had to be participating.

Unwittingly, Amanda emerged from her reverie as the minister entered. She looked around as hurried footsteps became audible. It was them – Derek and his family who walked straight down the left-hand aisle hoping to find an empty pew before they reached the front where the choir was seated.

To-day he would see her. She had her mind made up that she would speak to him – after all, that is why she had come to Church.

She thought to herself that, if she were ever asked why she attended Church these days, she would honestly have to admit that it was in the hope of seeing Derek.

As the worship progressed, she found herself automatically or mechanically standing for the hymns, sort of belatedly following the family, because her mind and eyes were expectantly on Derek. In the brief interval following the reading of the church intimations, shew was rewarded. Derek turned his head and scanned the congregation. Momentarily he stopped, and with the slightest of smiles half-acknowledged her. She would swear to that – and she never heard another word during the remainder of the service.

She imagined herself at the Youth Club excursion, rambling over the fields hand in hand with Derek, climbing together up the green slope towards the cliff edge. There they would throw themselves down on the grass and talk about what they were going to do with their lives. All the colours seemed more real and the sky bluer, the grass greener, and sounds more alive, both near and distant. It was there, she told Derek that she was hoping to follow nursing as a career, and Derek revealed that he felt God was calling him to enter the Church. That was why he worshipped every Sunday.

It was exciting to know they were both dedicated to helping their fellow man, and they both believed their lives were planned for them by God.

Amanda no longer thought only about herself and Derek; now she was encompassed and engulfed by something greater, more than an idealism, a real adventurous upsurge of her spirits which elevated her on to the unknown. It was a wonderful contemplative experience. She loved it, but could her dream become a reality? As God made them He would mate them.

9

Second Birthday

"Do you know when your second birthday is?" he questioned me.

"I'm sorry – what was that?" I replied, being at a loss of understanding.

With a deliberate and confident tone he repeated the question. "Do you know when your second birthday is? I do," he added.

Suddenly now its significance occurred to me. We had been travelling on the train for half an hour, seated opposite, silent strangers, when I prompted conversation by offering him my well-read *Telegraph*.

That one little act had encouraged him into some articulation. We talked generally for a little while; then he volunteered information on his journey which was to allow him to attend a religious rally. I had no reason for terminating the conversation, even though I obviously could discern the direction it was going. Then he made the observations already detailed.

"I suppose," I said, "that you're committed to the new charismatic movement?"

"I know what you mean," he replied, "albeit along with millions you erroneously apply that title."

"Well, what I was saying was that you were not in one of the mainstream traditional Churches."

"So be it – but let me tell you that, in my Church,

what you imply as the 'charismatic', we have been exercising so for nearly two thousand years. We were the
first Church and haven't changed since the day of
Pentecost."

"Do you have to go to your church to be with Christ
again as at Pentecost?" I asked.

"No, it's not like that – ever since I was saved – that
day when I went down on my knees and asked Christ
to come into my life – He has been with me.

"You see there was a time when I spent all my money
and my time gambling. If you had wanted to get hold
of me, I was at the race-track, failing that the 'bookies'.
It was great while it lasted, or so I thought. There was
a crowd of us, and we would have a good drink or two.
But, after a few years of that, I had nothing to show for
the years spent in a steady job – a very secure office one
at that too. I suppose I had an underlying sense of
unease or of frustration because anything I won, I
spent: but not on myself. No, I could manage with two
pairs of shoes and about four or five shirts at the most.
As long as I paid my digs and sent the odd present
home to my mother, and dropped in to see her and my
father occasionally everything on the surface seemed
all right.

"But after I'd been going with Hilary for a year, it all
came to a head. She more than put her foot down. Her
father was a man of God, and I soon saw there would
be no Hilary for me unless I changed my ways.

"And I did change. I remember that wonderful day
. . . that day I was born again – that day I was baptised
with the Holy Ghost. So my Saviour is with me all the
time; I don't have to go to church to be with Christ. I go
because there I can meet with other true believers and
kindred spirits; and there and then it's like Pentecost
again when God manifests himself – some will speak in

tongues and others interpret. In fact many of the gifts of the Spirit will be manifested."

"The latter point is interesting," I interjected, "because there are diverse opinions on that. One denomination, originating in Scotland and now presently active in Northern Ireland and North America, believes that the gifts of the Spirit died with the first century Apostles, and one might suspect that, with that attitude and belief, perhaps miracles too. It would be reasonable then for us to expect that they would put more emphasis on their own efforts, but what we find is exactly the opposite. They withdraw from pertinent issues in society, holding to historical attitudes which have no relevance to-day."

"I know about them," he replied, evading a direct critical response except to say that. "No wonder they have dwindling and decaying congregations and churches!

"It's not a matter of attitudes or tradition," he continued, "it is one of experience and knowledge. Some refuse to see, but I'm glad to say many others have brought light into the mainstream churches: who have had to wrestle with disbelief and even downright opposition, but have kept steadfastly to what they knew to be true.

"I go to church because there God so evidently shows Himself and I want to share in it and thank Him publicly for what He has done for me. Yes, I am saved, and I am not afraid to admit it. I believe – I know.

"God made me, Christ redeemed me and the Holy Ghost has sanctified me."

As the train slowed to a stop, "This is where I get off," he quietly added. "I would have liked to tell you more, but at least you know why I go to where I'm going."

"I would urge more people to go to church where they too can receive the 'Second Blessing'".

10

The Almanac of Time

Ronnie Davies was fortunate to be endowed with a good tenor voice, and, like his father before him, it seemed natural and obvious that he should join the chapel choir.

He knew that some of the worshippers never gave a moment's thought to the choir, to the work and preparation that was required. He knew, however, that, if for some reason the choir were to boycott the service, everyone would soon realise its importance. There were many congregations, however, which did not have choirs, and a few with not even a musical instrument to lead and support the praise. He had been to churches which didn't even sing hymns or any spiritual songs, where only the sacrosanct Psalms of David were the vocal music. He knew there were even assemblies of Christians who never sang anything – no music, vocal or otherwise at all.

Ronnie couldn't understand people like that, but it didn't worry him and he wouldn't disparage them. Nevertheless, he knew he went to his Methodist Chapel on Sundays because he had a very important part to play in the service. It was his duty, and he felt his presence was essential. The minister had always instilled into the choir-members the importance of their position and the need for regular attendance at practice.

So, with a mixture of apprehension and expectation, he made his way to the hall to the first meeting and practice with the new organist and choirmaster whom he was secretly hoping would not start auditioning.

Ronnie had been a devoted, dedicated member for thirty years and had seen off three organists and choirmasters, but he had to admit that his voice wasn't what it used to be.

As Ronnie entered the hall, one glance told him that all the regular members were there. The new choirmaster, after being introduced, opened his remarks by saying it would take him some time to get used to his team and how, as he was the goalkeeper and captain, he could see everything in front of him. He would see their strengths and weaknesses. Ronnie thought that he wasn't using an appropriate metaphor; never mind, as long as his music was good, why bother about his English.

The new organist, Evan Jones, did know his music and possessed all the desirable qualifications, including affiliation to the Royal College of Church Music. Evan had performed publicly, playing organ recitals, fugues, chorales, cantatas and other classical works by Bach, Mozart and others. His experience and repertoire was not limited to Psalms and hymns, or the Wesleyan style and arrangements of praise, which was often basic four part harmony, and simple to any qualified keyboard player. Being very catholic in his taste of religious music, he enjoyed cantatas, plainchant, pastorals and the great choral works of Handel and Beethoven.

The Psalter and Hymnal were the beginning, not the end, of Evan's church music. He knew of the great wealth of tunes, chants and liturgical items, melodies and harmonies, sacred words and poems which encompassed these and other publications, golden treasuries of inheritance from centuries of believers. Many of these he loved and cherished.

Evan Jones commenced by saying that on this first night he just wanted to talk, and asked everyone present to feel free to join in the conversation. Before closing, he wanted them to sing once only each of the proposed Sunday praise. He didn't intend tonight to make any comments.

As he continued to talk, Ronnie realised this choir-master was going to be different. Coming through was the conviction that Evan Jones believed in what he was doing, and that he was doing it to the glory of God.

The new organist went on to say about the Psalmody and Hymnal that nowadays their use required a great deal of consideration and under-standing when it came to interpretation and presentation with regard to accompaniment. The congregation had to be led, but in a way they could best follow. He also intended to introduce Gospel Spirituals and many new hymns in modern rhythms, including rock. He wanted the choir members to enjoy themselves, but always never to forget why they were where they were on Sunday. The music and their singing must be alive and assist the worship. Since all types and ages of people were in the congregation, this meant that the choir would not please everyone all the time.

He was not expecting the standard of oratorios, but to read and sing descant and counterpoint was neces-sary. Apart from accompaniment, the choir had to perform anthems, carols and classical songs on special occasions, but the Introit would not be a regular feature. He explained that he accepted the life of church organist and choirmaster because he felt that whatever talent he possessed was God-given and therefore should be used in God's work.

Ronnie and the older members needed no reminding. It was part of their life in the valley for as far back as they could remember. Their social and cultural life was awakened, nourished and sustained by their religious beliefs of Methodism. Their life had consisted of the coal mine and the chapel, and, although he had never been to the Eisteddfod himself, he had been involved in many competitive church concerts, which were a great feature of Welsh life. Then there was Dylan. He might not agree with Dylan, but he was proud of him. Dylan was of his time and knew and understood the people. Ronnie had experienced the bad times common to all the valleys and industrial areas – Rhondda, Merthyr Tydfil, Ebbw Vale and others, the unemployment and poverty, the accidents and disasters in the pits, the hardship and adversity throughout all of which the amicable, good fellow-feeling and camaraderie of genuine friendly neighbours and relations articulated in song, made life worth living and enjoyable. Praise to the Lord washed away more than sin, providing exhilaration even mirth and cheer, to gladden and elate the heart.

Ronnie's favourite hymn was Charles Wesley's great and well-known one:

"Love Divine, all loves excelling,
Joy of heaven, to earth come down,
Fix in us Thy humble dwelling,
All Thy faithful mercies crown:
Jesus, Thou art all compassion,
Pure, unbounded love Thou art;
Visit us with Thy salvation,
Enter every trembling heart."

Ronnie had thought he had heard it all, but this choir-master was different – he had never heard it put that way before,

Evan Jones spoke not only from knowledge and experience, but also with conviction: he didn't have the parochial attitudes of his predecessors. If he could play as well as he could speak, then they were all in for an inspiring time. Ronnie was already looking forward to Sunday. This Even Jones might be the man to bring some life back into the chapel.

11

To the Ends of the Earth

"Would you tell me about your religious experience and why you go to Church?" I asked my lady acquaintance.

We had boarded the bus at the same stop and, having known her slightly over the past ten years as one who lived in the same neighbourhood and who perhaps occasionally exchanged friendly words when passing in the street, I sat beside her. Little conversation took place until she purchased her ticket. Surprisingly to me, she was going to the terminus which was in an outlying town – a forty-minute journey. I suppose that was what prompted me into conversation with her. She said she was going to Church. I must have said five-thirty in the evening was an unusual time for setting out for worship. Not to her, she had replied, after her experience – any time, any place.

"I was a fairly regular Church attender for most of my life. I never asked myself why I should be a member of my particular Church, being the Church of England denomination, and never gave a thought as to why I should be going at all. I never questioned anything, possibly I never absorbed enough to pose a question. Looking back now, it all seems so passive, so lacking in vitality. Then there was this evangelical mission, which lasted two weeks during which fringe meetings took place. I still don't know who were supposed to be the leaders. It seemed as if the mission itself had got out of control and was itself racing away, accelerating, increasing its own momentum by the numbers of people who climbed aboard.

"I found myself at several evening sessions where only small groups of say between ten and twenty were present, but there was much talk and many questions. I remember one man was asked if he knew the Holy Ghost, and he replied he'd never heard of it. This man was well known to me and he sat usually across the aisle from me on a Sunday morning. One evening, I was invited to a group and I learned of the word 'charismatic'. Later in the evening, we sat in a circle, and starting with the leader, everyone had to say something which would help the evening along spiritually. One felt there was a Supernatural Presence.

"As each took it in his or her turn, and as around the circle the progression moved towards me, I felt a tingle at the back of my neck. I couldn't testify to anything, and yet felt some kind of intimidating force of emotion impelling and urging me on. I had always believed in God, but they were asking me now to proclaim it publicly. When it came my occasion, I remained silent. Later I was sorry. On being challenged, I had failed the test. I suppose I was afraid, as I didn't know what I was letting myself in for. Not long afterwards, however, I had a second chance, when I learned of the gifts of the Spirit and the fruits of the Spirit. Hands were laid on me and I was changed."

"Changed," I questioned, "and that is why you now travel ten miles across the city to go to Church?"

She quietly intervened, "I should have said 'healed'. You see, for years I had been crippled with arthritis, but Jesus Christ, through the vicar, healed me – yes, in a flash! Oh! I know we all have our own ideas about faith healing.

"Some are healed – others are not, but many of the latter approach life anew with a more positive attitude to their illness. Some people might say it is only suggestibility that gets results. I know how I used to be, I know how I am now. Wouldn't you travel ten miles weekly to worship your God if you had been healed?"

Looking into her eyes, I couldn't find anything to say at first. There was no reply to that. Personally, I would have journeyed a hundred and ten miles. Then, not in a flippant sense, but because I thought she was expecting a response from me, "You are fortunate that you live near Manchester, which has such a good bus service."

"Yes, perhaps," then she added quickly, "but the way I feel I would travel to the ends of the earth, to thank the Lord for his grace and favour towards me. It is more than being cured of a painful affliction; that was only the beginning. My eyes, ears, mind and heart were opened to appreciate and value all that I do have – all that He has bestowed on me. That also includes assurance, joy, peace and trust. What can I give God in return? One day in the week?"

She looked at me earnestly as she spoke rhetorically and then I realised again that one never knows what depth of love and faith is grounded in individual people.

12

More Ways than One

Walter Banks had never given one thought as to why he was a regular church-goer. From his early days he had attended Sunday services in St. Cuthbert's Anglican Church with his parents. He was an only child, and his father had died in the year when he himself was leaving school to be admitted as an apprentice to a local accountant. It was a lonely period in his life with a new awareness of a responsibility to his mother. He often looked back on that burdensome time.

He vowed to his mother that he wouldn't go off to work abroad or even too far away from her, that he wouldn't emigrate to leave her in any distress. He had not regretted it. His life from then on had been built around the Church with a strong belief in God.

He learned of, and wondered in awe at the great and glorious history of the Christian Church, and how even today it cannot escape from its past. All that has gone before is part of us without our knowing it. That inheritance which derives from the Anglicans is one to cherish, and he never once questioned the Protestant ethic. He knew he owed a great debt to his predecessors, and was occasionally haunted by an unpaid gratitude to the past. In his eyes, the Common Book of Prayer was an essential part of his religious life. It helped him immensely, and he often thought of the poverty of the nonconformists who had no formal liturgical written guide.

To-day he led his own family into the church. It was a visiting vicar who was officiating this morning, and, after the customary format of hymns and prayers, he embarked on his sermon with the early introduction of autobiographical preambles. One of these struck home with Walter – namely that the vicar too had been an only child and in his late teens had lost his father. Walter became more attentive to what was to follow.

The text was from that part of St. Mark's gospel commonly referred to as 'The rich young Ruler'. This didn't apply to me, Walter thought, or did it? Perhaps there was more ways than one of being rich?

That's what the sermon implied. Is it correct and fair to twist words and impose a different interpretation than the accepted standard? What are "great possessions", because "who then can be saved?"

By the time the preacher had finished, Walter was still turning that one point over in his mind. He had been brought up in a Christina home and had had a happy childhood. He had a good education and, although there was that little time of sadness, he had had an enjoyable happy youth with many young friends.

He was married to a capable and beautiful woman who took pride in looking after their two children. His job was interesting and rewarding. He owned his own home and car, and had many genuine friends, especially in the Church. His family as himself had been blessed with good health. Because he dwelt on what was wholesome and not the sordid or vulgar, he possessed a positive optimistic and healthy outlook on life. He had not sought happiness but had found well-being.

He was unbelievably content. He had little money in the bank, but surely he was rich. By to-day's standards, by any standards, he was rich.

Now he knew why he attended Church every Sunday, but more important why he would continue to do so. The God he knew was the Man of history, of parts of the Bible and of a Sunday. Walter had everything a man wanted. Everything, that is, except the real living God whose wealth knew no bounds. Could he have everything and Jesus Christ too? Perhaps life wasn't going to be so easy from now on. Could it be that any kind of richness or wealth is not necessarily inherited but can be acquired especially if you have "inside information"? That was why he was attending Church. He would have to learn more about the Bible, and deliberate on the readings in the service. He would have to purchase notes on daily Bible readings. Perhaps joining a Bible Class would help, or even a distance learning course?

The Bible as he understood the Old Testament was a history of the Jewish Religion, of men developing a God-fearing conscience, of men with imaginations and prophetic vision, of men who had common sense and good self-esteem, of men who understood the value of poetry and songs, of men who while suffering understood prayer, redemption and faith and how all this relates to the New Testament.

He had to admit that for years there were many passages of the Bible which meant nothing to him. They were too difficult to have any meaning without some knowledge of their origins and authors. As a book, it is full of analogies, paradoxes, rhetorics and myths, which are now confusing, but were meant to be illuminating and effective. But hadn't he been told often enough before by his minister to look on the Bible as a whole? It didn't matter if there were certain stories which were hard to believe – what mattered was to discover and understand the underlying values – the importance of man, his spirit, the victory of good over evil, an understanding and knowledge of God.

A short Bible history, or some kind of abridged Authorised Version, would get him started. There were other translations easily available and cheaply priced, such as the New English; Good News; Moffat's; The Living Bible and New International, some in paperback. A concordance would be useful. He would purchase one of those Bibles which had the words of Jesus printed in red. All this must surely help him to know whom he was worshipping, and give him more reasons for going to Church.

13

Sunday is Sunday
is Sunday

To be a Christian is a real thing in my life, so where else would I go on a Sunday other than to worship God in his Church?

I have professed my faith in Christ. He is my Saviour, so I can take my place there on a Sunday and be numbered among the believers. Church membership means church attendance. You have your adherents and nominal Christians there on Sunday too, but I would venture to say that although their membership doesn't count for much, their presence is important.

Of course, most people are interested in the Church for baptism, marriage and funerals, but then again the question is 'why?' Why do they religiously subscribe lip-service to these Christian sacraments and rituals when they won't accede to the one and only commitment – that is to Jesus Christ?

It is beyond my understanding why so many of these people go to church at all.

But for real Church members who attend regularly, there is a joining or fusing together in the fellowship of the Church. As members of one family, we belong to each other and are there to care for, support and encourage one another. Since I confessed my sins by a personal act of faith, I am admitted to the full privileges of Church membership.

This means loyalty to fellow Christians and by a life of prayer, fellowship, witness and Sunday worship identification with my Saviour.

I don't have to give reasons for going to my church.

It is only when I am actually present in church that I know for sure why I am there; only when I am in the act of worship amidst all the believers that I have that feeling of belonging – a deep sense of reassurance. Then I only hope I have ears to hear, a mind to understand and a heart to respond to the word of God: that word introduced in the Catechisms, the Creeds and the Sermon on the Mount.

The first Church I attended was a small tabernacle in a working class district of Liverpool. It was there I learned the fundamentals. It was there I learned to stand up for my faith. There, where the Irish, Welsh and English meet in an amalgam condensed by the addition of other foreign overseas sects and nationalities as a penalising consequence of being once a great port, I spoke my testimony for the first time.

Since then I have married, moved across the country to a new employment in East Yorkshire and transferred to an established church. Bible study at a mid-week meeting has finally resulted in my serious consideration of full-time ministry. So another reason for being at the Sunday services is to learn – especially from the sermon – and observe the style of preaching. One address recently was on praying and why we don't engage in it more often. Why we are neglectful. Why we must work on it daily. Meditation generally helps to create the proper attitude before any devout supplication to God, whether private or part of public liturgy.

Many voice the opinion that invocation to them is a compulsion, which could be described as intuitive, but then there would be no free will or freedom of choice if intuition were naturally involved. The sermon went on to explain the biblical basis of fasting, and how that has become a lost art. Much of the apparent ineffectual prayer must be attributed to the absence of fasting in conjunction therewith.

How many people fast nowadays? How many Christians fast nowadays? Can fasting deepen one's prayer life, strengthen one's relationship with God, deepen one's realisation of spirituality?

There is clear affirmative and unequivocal evidence in the Bible. But again, the other important matter is the one of keeping the Sabbath holy.

Sunday just wouldn't be Sunday if I weren't present at the church service. I go because I feel the need to make the day different. And God knows how the sanctity of the Sabbath has been eroded by modern attitudes in society.

I look forward to Sunday for the opportunity of having a day of difference. A day that is more slowly paced, when you can attend your House of God knowing the day is different; the people you meet are different; the thoughts you have are different; the songs you sing are different. The day on which people freely and overtly give instead of receiving. The language you hear and conversation are different.

At least, I want to put my God first. If, after worship, I want to participate in sport or recreation, then I can do so without any qualms of conscience or reproaching myself in any way.

Many secular activities are freely patronised on a Sunday now, but many people still want Sunday to be different and live accordingly. Its desecration has gone far enough, resulting in a large degree of irreverence, but some would look on a free-for-all Sunday as an intrusion into its day of quietness and privacy, but others enjoy the day shopping.

'The Sabbath was made for man' wasn't it?

Sunday is, or should be, a family day, with preferably outdoor activities, increasing the quality of family life, or a day to relax, read, converse and if possible enjoy the company of like-minded friends.

14

Remember Adlestrop?

We can trace our family tree in this area right back to 1680, but not necessarily in the village itself. As a young girl, I can remember being told to believe we had an important part to play in the local community. It was both my heritage and my inheritance to live actively in the neighbourhood, supporting and encouraging all aspects of church and secular life. Our family has been patriarchal in its relationship with all others around here. We have a whole history of successful farming, not to mention the contribution made to the military profession when the need arose. Of course, I've always considered it a privilege to help in the parish, and all during my own considerable years I can say it has all been very worthwhile. You can see our family's memorial tablets on the church walls and we possess the only vault under the south transept.

A varied social life exists around our beautiful old church here where you will see me regularly on Sundays.

It has a certain significance both from an historical and architectural aspect, in the village. It is a little like Adlestrop, the church I mean, not the village, with its stonework, the fifteenth century tower, the two-faced clock, its Gothic windows, and commemorative gates. You must remember Adlestrop I'm sure? Our own church has its special significance to all around the environment here. It always was, and remains to-day, the centre of our lives.

The rector and his family are such splendid people; it's such a joy to see them every Sunday, when if I hadn't the church to go to I really wouldn't know what to do.

Everyone's so nice to me now, even though with my tweeds I'm just an old eccentric lady to many of the young people whom I just love seeing with all my friends on a Sunday.

I have so many pleasant memories especially of those long, hot sunny cloudless timeless summer Sundays, of a world that is sadly disappearing, when, after a week's hard work, the parishioners gathered in a devout friendly good-neighbourly way for worship. Even though there was a high blue sky, it was always cool inside the church. I think somehow that helped our piety and reverence.

In those days faith was strong, and time ran more slowly.

England was more English than it is now.

I suppose being an island we could keep the world out; being a village we could turn our backs on the worst of the industrial revolution, and that natural repudiation helped the spirituality of the community, perhaps assisted our religious aspirations.

In those days, before the affluent society, before the emancipated woman, before television, and before the welfare state, before the collapse of traditional values, we were content with our simple faith, bearing our burdens and sorrows with fortitude, caring more for each other, hoping to grow in grace, and glad to be church-goers.

Nowadays, although still content with our Anglican

faith, we seem to require peripheral activities to supplement the morning worship. Of course, most local events are traditional and the village wouldn't be the same without the church fête we hold annually. It is such a joyous occasion.

That always was, and always will be, a day of importance in my church life, and now it seems that my good attendance at worship is rewarded by my still being well enough to live and see and participate in another fête with all the planning and preparation for weeks before. The rector's wife always allocates the various stalls, but for years the 'plants' has been my private domain to run and organise. It's a red letter day. A day of fun and merriment, amusement and entertainment. A village fête is an English institution and the word itself summons up thoughts of white tents and new-mown grass lawns, afternoon teas, books and cake stalls, children's games, ices and lemonade, music and laughter. I remember the first time we planned and auctioned off some livestock, and introduced the wheel of fortune. Was the rector going to have a change of heart at the last moment and prohibit these 'morally doubtful' activities? It was all for a good cause – harmless, but more exciting fun than the croquet or darts' competition. He endeared himself to all of us by sportingly insisting on opening the bidding and buying five chances at the wheel!

That soon enlivened the occasion and put everyone in a good humour. I remember many such halcyon days. Now I like to encourage the continuance of the fête and other activities, both sacred and secular. That too is part of my Sunday worship.

But the stone-built church itself, the inside of which is simply but beautifully adorned lends timeless meaning to us all.

15

Where There's a Will

Harry could still remember quite vividly the years of depression in the thirties. He could still see his mother, aged before her time, working her fingers to the bone to feed, care for and rear her three children, while his father lay long in his bed, or stood around idly at the street corner. Any money his father ever had, went on drink and the horses. His mother did charring jobs to earn a little. It hadn't all been an unhappy time, but, when he was eighteen years old, having turned his back on school four years since, he still had no permanent job. Fortunately, he enjoyed reading and spent hours absorbed in books. He remembered that particular September when his mother came to him.

"Harry, I'm not so well and fit as I used to be, and might not be able to keep working this winter. I'm worried – things will be bad for all of us. You're the eldest and you have to do something. There's only one person I know who could help – your uncle William. I know I haven't seen my brother for years since we came to live here. It's true he was a stickler for right and wrong, and he never liked your father, but he's got a good heart. He'll help. He's got a good job with the Post Office. Would you go and see him? You have to for my sake. See what he says."

Harry thought Glasgow in those days was at the same time both a great and a terrible place. If you lived in the centre, it was vibrant with people and life. Transport was cheap. The trams and the subway were always crammed with passengers, mostly under-nourished and not too elegantly dressed. It was the first of the "No Mean Cities".

That night, in late September when Harry chose to visit his uncle in an outlying town, it turned out a windy and wet one. He had to walk a good part of the journey, even though he went by tram and bus as much as his pocket would permit. A ghastly sight he must have looked as he squelched up the stairs to the tenement flat.

What William Grant saw in the dim light when he opened the door was a young man with a cloth cap, trousers and jacket, open-necked shirt and gym shoes all dripping wet. Taken aback, and more than slightly apprehensive when confronted by the strange and even sinister looking person, all he could say was, "Yes?" to which the wan and gaunt figure answered.

"I'm Harry, Uncle William – you know – your nephew, Harry Dowds."

"Harry! Come in – you're soaked to the skin – something wrong, is your mother all right?" regaining himself with composure.

Harry looked back on those days and said to himself that nobody nowadays really knows what it's like to be down and out.

That evening his uncle William rigged him out with some of his own clothes. In particular he remembered the raincoat was a real blessing, and luckily he had the same size in shoes. Uncle William managed to arrange a job – only as a labourer in the Post Office Telephones, but with his love of books, Harry taught himself many things. Six months later, he was converted and joined the Brethren.

Neither a drinker, nor a smoker, he was able to contribute substantially to the household and proved a great source of joy and comfort to his mother.

There was, however, a sad, bitter episode involving his father, who took everything and gave nothing, except to scoff at Harry's good fortune and new-found faith. Harry prayed about his problem, and God made him "weep his pints like you and me." He saw the irony in that, even in those old days of poverty, his father was never aggressive or cruel to any of them. He was then just a pathetic figure of a man, a failure, accepting with docile resignation his fate. Years on the dole had knocked the heart out of him. But now Harry saw in him a jealousy and envy, by way of which he was taking the brunt in verbal abuse.

Next would come violence, and his mother would be vulnerable. For her sake he left the house, and started a new life in lodgings. He often saw his mother and donated what he could to alleviate her financially. He never looked back. He willingly toed the doctrinal line of practices and procedures, and the pastor was good to him. With the outbreak of war, the pastor pushed him into other opportunities and he soon had a good white-collar job, and was a reliable member of the Hall. He had been saved in more ways than one. He was surprised how resolute and resourceful he had become.

He would never miss a Sunday to worship. Many a time he had been asked to speak at a variety of venues, but it wasn't in his nature to propound his faith publicly. He wasn't particularly eloquent, but in any case he didn't feel the need to start 'Bible-thumping'.

He was more than grateful for what grace God had bestowed on him, and with quiet undemonstrative resolution he lived on in faith. He looked back on how far he had come and, without fear, had hope for the future. Sad it was, he thought, that his mother never did see Uncle William. She was worn out and done aged fifty-five, and died comfortably in hospital. He had held her hand right to the end.

16

Tate and Barbican

My wife is a fairly devout person and goes to church regularly. I accompany her, or you might say I take her and I go because she goes. I would rather attend than be left to do all the chores around the house and prepare the Sunday lunch every week. Of course, I take my turn at that too to give her a break, because Sunday morning can be one of her busiest in the week, having to leave the house at twenty minutes to eleven to arrive in time, and not be rushing down the aisle as the congregation is singing the first hymn. But when you examine it, you'll find many individuals attend church because of someone else, perhaps just to please. Children go with their parents. Grandmothers might be taken along by their daughter or granddaughter. I know one man who goes because he has to transport his folks as they have no car; a lot better than another I know who deposits his mother at the church door, then drives off home to read the Sunday papers. Then there are a good number who are bussed in free of charge from some of the new outlying housing estates. I wonder how many would take the trouble to find their own way to town if this service were not provided. Some widows, then again, would make an arrangement to call on a friend who could accompany them to church.

Now many of these types of people are attending worship in their own right, but some go along only in a supportive way. Nevertheless, they are also to be admired and respected, and form an important category of worshippers. You could call them adherents.

It was when I spent a year on voluntary work overseas amongst people of varying religions that I learned to care for people without asking too many questions.

Left to themselves, the nationals co-operated with each other to a surprising degree, and only when religious or political advocates intervened did you see introspection, fear and bigotry, not to mention superstition. In that year, I experienced several revealing, exhilarating spiritual experiences and I was nowhere near a church.

To-day I can experience and absorb a spiritual effect from a Rachmaninoff concert at the Barbican, or at an afternoon at the Tate with the French Impressionists: an unexplained elation, which fathers a pleasant surmise.

There must be thousands of spiritual experiences outside the realm of religion, happening to millions of people every day. But religion would claim that perhaps it wasn't possible. However, to my way of thinking there could be numerable varieties of spiritual experience, if people would only recognise them for what they are.

I'm in the teaching profession and we try to inculcate decent values and basic religious beliefs with advice and instruction, but experience will be the great teacher for most. Detailed religious education is something for which in school we don't have time. In a pluralistic society we need to teach more understanding, and because of the number of races now living in Britain not to mention the endless list of branches of the Christian faith, we cannot be too dogmatic about God and how to worship him.

And it's not in my school curriculum to explain the difference between Jehovah's Witnesses, Mormons, Congregationalists, Christian Scientists, Baptists, Brethren, Quakers, etc., etc., not forgetting the established branches of the faith.

As a teacher I like to read widely. One particular passage is very meaningful to me: "He is not a philosopher like the rest, he is a philosopher who has seen the world."

I do not know the source of this quote, but it was spoken of Schopenhauer the German thinker. It means that his ideas came out of his contact with the world. Some philosophers think in their study-rooms, far removed from the hurly-burly of the world, and pronounce their findings worked out in solitude. Schopenhauer faced the human situations, the good and the bad, the agony and the ecstasy, the happiness and the suffering and indeed went through such things himself. And out of all this came his system of philosophy. There is no hope for philosophers who will not face the facts: to give any interpretation of human life one must get to know it; and to talk about the world, one must live in it. What are people like? What kind of world do we inhabit? These are the great questions, not only for the philosopher, but also for the preacher. Instead of starting with theology and then attempting to fit the experience into it, much better to start with human experience and then try to find a theology that interprets it. The theology of the market-place must always better the theology of the classroom.

My wife has her own reasons for church-going, and I would neither intrude into her privacy nor be so presumptuous as to ask what these are.

I have several reasons, one being that it is important that the schoolchildren should see their teacher worshipping in common with others, well away from the scholastic environment. I would then find that these young folk could be more easily disciplined because they are quick to see a flaw or inconsistency in their elders' reasoning. Just because they accompany their parents to the House of God doesn't make them less critical – not in any way. And, if I'm honest, I think at times when I attend church that I adopt an attitude myself; where I'm hoping I won't hear anything in the preacher's address, as such would diminish spirituality.

Over the years I have learned Bible verses which keep coming back into my consciousness and which are of importance to me and are spiritually uplifting.

"I am the bread of life."

"Rejoice evermore, Pray without ceasing, In every thing give thanks."

"With men it is impossible, but not with God: for with God all things are possible."

These words encourage and reinforce my faith and self-esteem.

17

Time and Tide

Billy Nixon was just at the age when he was developing an attitude to life, a way of looking at things. Past sixteen years, he had progressed from the Sunday School to the Bible Class which was held prior to Sunday morning worship. The previous year he had enjoyed the class under old Mr Benson, a man devoid of any pride or presumption. Billy, even at his young impressive age, knew that it wasn't so much what Mr Benson said by way of precept, but more by the way he spoke and also by his example of patience, friendliness and humour. Mr Benson, no matter what the Bible text was for any particular day, always seemed to finish with the Beatitudes. He knew them backwards and seemed to live his life by them, and on them he placed great emphasis. It was Mr Benson who had awakened in Billy a feeling of well-being, and kindled a spirit of religious adventure. For didn't Benson know also the biographies of all the great Christian men and women of the nineteenth and twentieth centuries, who were giants in the world, and the results of whose lives were still to be seen.

Billy could see how, in this one realm of education, there was a parallel with the days of, and before, the Greeks and Romans, when boys and girls gathered in the market-place and learned by listening to their elders speaking and discussing all current matters. They learned in these days without books, just listening to travellers, sailors, scholars or priests and committing to memory what was considered important.

Communication and inspiration were everything. He thought how well Mr Benson would have filled that role of the wise knowledgeable scholar.

Before Mr Benson's class, he went to Sunday School and Church as a matter of form – he was expected to go, but during the past year he actually looked forward to attending. His experience and knowledge of people, the Church and God was developing. He often thought had God a plan for him? This year the Bible Class leader, Harry Robson, was even better than Mr Benson, and was showing Billy several avenues to follow.

First, there was great enthusiasm and friendship amongst all the teenagers who were encouraged to be open and frank. Billy could really say that he enjoyed going to the class and the church. Harry Robson was showing them and telling them of present day living Christians – young girls and boys, women and men in sport and entertainment, who were prepared to stand up for their principles.

Then Billy learned of other young groups of Christians with whom were held fellowship rallies. Billy never realised there were so many books available for study, or just general reading, for young people – and magazines too. The Scripture Union publications were interesting and helpful. More and more of what the parson said at the service was Billy able to put together and assemble a meaning and purpose.

He felt with all the fun at the class, and the Friday and Saturday activities – picnics, sponsored walks and barbecues, that the world was a wonderful place. It was good to be part of a crowd who knew where they were going – there was a common direction and purpose. He seemed to get confidence and strength from the class.

It was great to be young, and to know everyone had the same belief in God. He felt wonderful and thought it would be great if he lived his life always on that plane.

But Billy was to go even higher. Harry Robson harnessed his enthusiasm, energy and commitment into social service.

On one evening each week Billy, with a friend, found himself visiting a hospital or an old people's home. They carried tape recorders and laptops, being allowed in certain circumstances to entertain or provide a messenger service. He didn't analyse it as a caring ministry. He didn't set about looking for spiritual and material needs to satisfy.

They were simply doing a little bit of good, and after Harry Robson had them going properly organised, he left them to it. But Billy did feel he was a disciple in the sense that he was learning a lot about the right things. He was working for God, but stopped short in thinking himself Christ's ambassador. But he felt he was heading that way. Worship on a Sunday was no longer a weekly ritual on its own, divorced from all other activities; it was just one of a number of other forms of worship in which he was participating. He attended church on a Sunday because he had found an exciting new dimension to his life, an idealism he didn't know before.

He was glad he was a Baptist, although he had no knowledge of other denominations. Yet he knew that his Christian friends, his preachers, guest speakers and visitors all possessed a vitality. He read that the Baptist Union was forward-looking and realistic in its attitudes to a changing society with the new world of lasers, computers, earth satellites, inter-planetary rockets and instant communications. The national leadership seemed to be strong and young, and with their sure solid faith were eager to embrace the scientific challenge of the present day.

The Baptists, he had heard, may be the first denomination to throw off completely its nineteenth century chrysalis and emerge the great missionary Church of the twenty-first century. The old forms of liturgy, the old forms of worship, the old formalism, the old methods of preaching, the old preachers, the old places of worship, the old hymns must make way for the new dynamic young Christians.

He identified himself as one of them. He was much involved with his God, his family and his community – and he enjoyed it.

18

Safe and Sound

I go to church, although not as often as I should, because it stands for a sureness that I constantly need in my own life. That sureness is my certain belief in God. Don't ask me what sort of God: I know only that Christ is there somewhere. I don't have time, and never did have time, to go into the 'ins and outs' of it all. After years of marriage, my man walked out on me and left me with three children to rear.

Their father had never been a member of the church. I was a communicant even though a poor attender, but I did manage to have the children baptised. So my pastor, who was very good to me at the time, encouraged the children to go to Sunday School: a business I've managed successfully to continue during the past ten years. People think once the divorce comes through, life can get back to some kind of normality.

It is not so. You always feel a bit of yourself is missing. Then again you are not the same as other families. You don't have a normal social life; at times, you don't have any social life.

Some people shun you, others are condescending and patronising. Of course, I could have gone home to my mother or lived with my sister in another town ten miles away, but that wouldn't have been fair on them. I might have done so but for my minister who helped me to find again a faith, not by running away, but by facing up to the reality. It's not easy having no man in the family, having no father for the children. It's been a struggle. And it's not easy going to church on your own, either.

There are, thank the Lord, in our church many decent, genuine and friendly members, who do live up to their beliefs. More often I would go on my own, leaving the youngsters at home in the evening, especially during the autumn or winter. You can slip in and out of church where the darkness envelops and hides you, and, though being alone, you feel safe. But then that's why I attend church. I feel safe there too.

Now I can understand why people retreat into solitariness. And you find them everywhere – in a flat in a high-rise block in the city, or in a remote cottage on an island, or just down any street in any town. Some are beyond the reach of anyone. They might not all be poor or old or handicapped. Some ironically may have reached the heights of public acclaim, but are now the forgotten cast-offs.

Without help from my parents, without assistance from the pastor and one or two neighbours and a few people in the church, I could not have made it, financially or otherwise. I don't know whether I would marry again. Once bitten . . . !

It was my pastor and the church members who roused me to action, who led me to have a better respect for myself, who helped me to find myself. I must admit it took him ages to get through to me, but he never gave up. It was he who listened, understood, encouraged and approved.

Now I lead as normal a life as is possible, having a part-time job where I have several friends; but without some sort of faith it would be extremely difficult. I have my children for company just now, but I often wonder what will happen to me when they reach adulthood. It's a thought on which I don't like to dwell.

Of course, when I couldn't go to church, the religious programmes on TV and the radio were a real comfort. Often a verse would stand out and I would grasp at it and memorise it, and when I was anxious and afraid I'd repeat to myself. "The Lord is my helper and I will not fear what man will do unto me" . . . "I will never leave thee nor forsake thee." To explain how hard and harrowing a time it has been, you have to understand I'm a West Indian who immigrated and settled here in London years ago. All around me were my own Nationals and that has been a blessing.

But by far the greatest impact on me has been what some might call the "second blessing". Our congregation is mainly people of Caribbean culture and origin, and we all feel blessed in some way or other. There is real rhythm in our worship. Gospel, spiritual and joyful happy songs are sung to the Lord as drums are beating, people spontaneously clapping, swaying and dancing in adoration and thanksgiving. I've seen three offerings being uplifted in one service that lasted two hours, with nobody wanting to rush away home.

That is what it means to worship in my church.

19

It Makes Sense

Church-going was never my forte – but I do go – not as much as I should. Being a business man, member of the local tennis and rugby club, Round Table and active committee man of the town's Chamber of Commerce, I work hard and play hard. My wife and I like a good time at the weekend, and there's nothing wrong with that. We do a lot of charitable work, as well as being right in the middle of the social swim.

We could be out three or four nights in the week, either in connection with my work or on charity affairs. I like to think of myself as a responsible member of society, able and willing to play my part in the voluntary organisations of which there seems to be no end. There is a tremendous length, breadth and height to the good work that is being accomplished in these fields – work that should be done by either the Government or the Church. There is no need for me to enumerate all these associations soliciting help – I couldn't anyhow. You will always have the under-privileged and under-nourished, the disadvantaged and discarded, the unfortunate and unwanted, so if we didn't have a caring, generous public giving of their time and money – the job of the clergy in this country would be a great deal more demanding than it is at present.

But then when, on buying the Sunday papers and

reading a few pages, I'm reminded of what a terrible world this is, I begin to think, without looking any further than our own country, of how standards have fallen in every walk of life.

There is a whole group of lazy layabouts living off the State, and it seems very few are prepared to accept any more the consequences of their own foolish actions. And there are all the abuses under the sun – child abuse, alcohol abuse, drug abuse; so much is seedy and sordid these days, both in fiction and fact. So young persons stepping out into this world, without any traditional moral values of their own, could be in for a confusing and troubled time. Therefore I pack my children off to Sunday School in order that they will learn at least some ethical principles. With nothing else on offer, Christianity is the only thing left for any of us.

I know that is putting it a bit low, but it makes sense.

It is not that I don't believe in God – or for that matter do believe in Him, but I hate to imagine what this country would be like without the Church. So it is really for the children's sake that I go. After all, I want them to grow up with some knowledge of ethics so that they don't flounder when they make their own way in life.

I also hope that I'm setting some kind of example to them which they will remember, as my dad did before me; showing them that being a member of the church and attending fairly regularly is not incompatible with being a competitive participant in the secular world.

We all have to live, and for most of us it takes quite an effort at times to survive while raising a family.

So I attend church with my wife and children, but really for my children.

Secretly, of course, I suppose I get a smug feeling of being one of the business community's leading sound family men.

There are many business men in our church so it doesn't do any harm to be one of them.

A few of these men, industrious and enterprising, have created wealth and employment in the town, helping others to improve their standard of living. They are doing this to the glory of God, perhaps indirectly, but none the less, making use of what talents they have to improve man's lot on His earth.

I've heard it said that it is not only ironic, but tragic, that the running of the business of the Church is left in the hands of men who, as seen by some, possibly serve God and Mammon. It is not a fair judgement, but it is understandable. But we could equally condemn the Christian who opts out of his responsibility, who has a disdain for success and wealth, of which he may have little, and then for the rest of his life lives off the charity of fellow Christians, because he is pursuing God's cause. Neither should he be judged.

Thankfully, in our church, we have a good mixture of people; and also a mixture of good people. There is one feeling above all that permeates through and that is the concern for, and the encouragement of, the young. I understand that it's been the policy of the Church to promote and elect into office family men; that is, men with young families.

The results are there to be seen. The children do not seem to be too distant from their elders. The children's talents in singing, music, reading and drama are supported and aided.

Children, as you know, through their friends can act as vehicles for introductions to people about whom you might never have entertained aspirations of knowing.

So it relates to the youngsters again, if I am to be really honest. Initially I go to church for their sake, but I am quite willing, there being no reluctance on my part. They will need all that they can learn on a Sunday, when they grow up and leave home to live on their own. I hope I may have helped them.

20

The Latest Fashion

When Maude was asked why she went to church, she said there were many reasons. She had many friends in the church and they all would meet socially. They were interested in each other, and in everyone else too – who married who – who was ill, etc. She said some would call it gossip. One of her great joys in attending church was looking at her own sex to see how they were attired. She knew men probably don't realise that women dress up primarily to show ostentatiously to other women.

She remembered the days when she would want to get to church to see what her dear friend Alice Driver's attire was like, what she had bought at the sales, and was exhibited for Maude's benefit. Nowadays, nobody hardly ever wears a hat. She thought that was sad. But there are the spring outfits, summer dresses and autumn coats to admire. It's nice to be noticed when you have a new suit on for the first time, and people generally are kind and complimentary. If, by chance, your friend doesn't acknowledge the fact that you are wearing something special, you ask yourself that perhaps you are being too presumptuous in thinking she is really your friend.

She liked to sit in the pew and slowly survey. It's an innocuous pursuit, but takes more effort now than when hats were 'all the go'. An unusual hat stood out sometimes outrageously. Of course, all this never detracted her from personal involvement in the service, but if the sermon was a bit boring and repetitive, she could always look around and search for the unexpected.

There was one woman in particular Maude admired; one woman of such elegance and good taste that Maude would love to copy and emulate. Anything she wore was made to look better and more expensive than it was – a quality and virtue envied by most women; but Maude wouldn't demean herself by imitating a younger woman. Maude knew also how mothers dressed up their daughters, even in this day at Easter services, with straw hats and coloured ribbons trailing half-way down their backs. It was heartening to see a mother's pride in her daughter, the natural feeling of human affection. They vied with each other in a truly friendly way for pride of place, when it came to turning out their daughters in dressing up for Church service. Maude loved the bright colours of children's dresses, but admitted she was more interested in the adults. Maude mused that church was as good a place as anywhere to see the up-and-coming fashions, and it was perhaps because of men's drab and uniform attire that women were conspicuous. Maude was convinced there was one good result from her absorbing interest; she would know at once if any of her friends were indisposed and unable to attend.

Maude's mind dwelt on some of the women in the church – how talented, how hardworking, how devoted. There was Mrs Drivers who, with her wardrobe, must have an entrée into a wholesale warehouse: it was known her husband worked in a big store in the city. Then there was Julie Roberts, a young capable woman who could make her way in life as a professional dressmaker. The clothes she tailored for herself and her daughter were splendid. And Marian Steele was a mystery – or was she? In winter rather dowdily dressed, but in spring and summer a revelation!

Of course, Maude knew she wasn't alone with these thoughts. It was both comforting and reassuring to know that her minister's wife was the most fashion-conscious of them all. With Maude it usually stopped with dresses and coats, but with the lady of the manse, shoes and hair styles were also a phobia. She was the only woman that all the others certainly looked to, and of them she was conscious. She was a woman's woman – a great asset to her husband and the church. It might be said she was "the cynosure of neighbouring eyes".

But Maude knew that the main concern of the minister's wife was for people. She it was who galvanised the congregation into a caring agency. She was a social worker before her marriage, after taking a degree in psychology and sociology. In those days, she was involved with handicapped people, then later with mental health and family problems. She was expertly equipped to organise a caring congregation. Her own personable character enabled her to enlist the loyalty of her eager voluntary assistants.

It was no longer social work, but Christian social witness, as a follow-up to her husband's intercourse with the parishioners in their spiritual demands. She taught them to use their God-given but human heal-ing potential, by way of speech and touch, and channelling and manipulating God's energy to help and comfort distressed souls who are unable to cope with life. And not only those in the congregation, but in outreach all who needed help as an expression of

Christ's compassion.

But Maude knew that they both prayed for contrition to accept anyone in any attire – everyone – with respect and humility.

Women are asserting themselves in the life of the Church. That's the latest fashion.

21

Why Not Every Day?

I attend my chapel very often indeed, and not just on Sundays. That's what I just cannot understand about the Protestant denominations: with the exception of their Cathedrals and the high Anglican buildings and the churches of a few enlightened clergy scattered throughout the country, their doors are barred and gates bolted six days in the week. I'm pleased I can go to my church any day, perhaps for mass or confession or just for quietness. I suppose I could say, "When I feel like it," but the motivation or prompting may be one of depression or exaltation. When women like I develop a habit of worshipping, then we don't wait for a feeling. We go because we've learned from the past that prayer and piety must be part of our lives.

It's the way I was reared, to believe without questioning – and I've been content with that.

There's always been advice and comfort at hand on a daily basis, if I needed it. But I think it's because I know that our local priests are interested in me as a human being, interested in my social and material welfare, that I go to my church. The clergyman knows me, so I don't have to pretend to be anyone but myself, and I find in our church a truly uplifting quietude, a real religious atmosphere telling me God is there. I don't worry about the Church as an institution –

whether it stands for or expresses the truth, but I know that I find God there. I live by it simply, and find comfort in it. The symbolism I find helpful, and in this day and age anything that helps one to remember God cannot be bad.

It does assist to focus your mind on your faith, and can help you to see beyond yourself. But my greatest blessing is this: for a good number of years past I've been looking after my invalid mother, and wouldn't want it any other way. But it's very constant work; day after day, night after night. There's only the two of us, and she is incontinent. She needs my help to get up and be dressed, even if only to sit in a chair all day gazing into the fire which I always have on for her even in the summer time. But it is trying. A social helper comes in only once a week. I can tell you it's a great relief to get out to do the shopping – an even greater one to escape to church and attend worship. I don't feel guilty leaving her to go to chapel – any time – any day. Although her mind wanders a bit, she does understand that much – God bless her. I don't know what I would do if I had nowhere to go for reassurance.

We receive regular letters every two months or so from my brother, who is in the Dominican Order in Nigeria, where he has spent the past ten years assisting in the creation of a monastery. His correspondence is both interesting and comforting to my mother and myself, but it is no substitute for live human contact.

He explains in writing how they are supportive to the local Catholic hospitals and churches, which are staffed by both national and international loyal believers of all colours and races. Nobody will ever appreciate, he says, the dedication and selfless devotion of the sisters, priests and lay people in whatever professional or technical capacity they serve.

Some day I would like to visit there and see him, and meet all his wonderful, colourful friends.

Meanwhile, I go to chapel and pray for him, the monks and the nuns and all the missionaries in his far-off African world. It is gratifying to learn of how many of our young people still go to Africa in order to assist in a variety of ways the church there which is now an important voice in the world.

Their devotion, dedication to work and worship continues every day of the week.

22

It's Political

I am one of those political animals. Ever since I was a youth, I liked the sound of my own voice and set my sail to get into Parliament. Concentrating on being articulate, because rhetoric can move mountains, I followed the way of School Debating Society, Students' Union and membership of the Liberal Party, and gained some standing in the local community as a councillor. So you see I've put my political future before anything – before money, or before a satisfying job, even before the family – yes, and perhaps before the Church. There is no point in being anything less than frank and honest. This may sound pompous, but I know my own ideas for changing society are to the benefit of all. These ideas are in themselves initially not only based on Christianity, but also the very essence of the social gospel that is preached in many places. You may say it is my religion. I do believe in God, but I also believe it's important for me to have the right image – the God-fearing, hard-working, caring, family man. I'll do anything to create that, and present myself in that vein to the people and the potential electorate – and that's one reason why you will see me attending worship regularly on Sundays. Of course, one also has to show a lead, especially in a small community. Some are born to lead – that may sound arrogant, but you have to face up to the facts. Out of the myriad types of people and from the vast range of social classes, there are really very few individuals prepared to put the well-being of others as a priority of their *raison d'être*.

You could say that, from a certain compassion, I do what I'm doing as I see the ordinary people being buffeted by life, being pulled this way and pushed that way. Due to their lack of education or common sense or whatever, they are exposed and are very vulnerable to the whims of others; being exploited and manipulated, not least by the media. Even the Church, generally speaking, has been guilty of this in the past, and could be so in the future. The Church in history had always a power base, and we all know how Christianity has been instrumental in improving man's lot on this planet. The Church, or its representatives, started education and hospitals or medical care, and was in there meeting man's basic needs. This seemed to stop at the beginning of the twentieth century in relation to the western civilised world. What present-day social, cultural or basic material need is the Church supplying to-day? It is no longer the authority it was. It has lost its power, but worse still it has lost its direction. Politics are what matter. The Christians have to reassert themselves and in what they believe through the ballot box.

The biggest blasphemy to-day is to say, "God's in His Heaven – All's right with the world."

The concept of changing men's hearts must not be a priority of the Church, nor a first tenet of doctrine in isolation. Men's needs, whatever they be, have to be ministered unto.

The Anglican Church, the most stable of England's institutions, whilst preserving the continuity of historical tradition with regard to spirituality, must surely now use its base to address the sociological problems of the day. It must have a political approach.

If my vocation is to help people, I need political power. It is necessary to meet as many as possible; which I can do on a Sunday morning. I also need the power that comes from quiet reflection. This I can also receive by Sunday worship. These are unconventional ideas perhaps, but then there's not much in life which is straightforward. Yet not so strange when you understand that many of the great Biblical leaders of Israel were both spiritual and political, and they were not democratic either.

"The men of new are like the men of old,
Of whom proud Sin has won and made decay
These same high virtues which today are told,
And taught to children twixt their sleep and play.
Why call them new and whisper it from grave to grave?
Why shout them from the pulpit high?
When all we need is action and the words,
The Church won't let our morals die.
Join with the State, work side by side,
Reveal to all a finer educational plan,
Often we have heard the death bells peal,
For Kingdoms, Churches, all – yet never Man.

My religious practice can be misunderstood and could be described as a masquerade and even heresy by some, but I make no apology. On the contrary, more church-going people must get into the political workplace and more politicians into the church.

Christians are being persecuted and their traditions and values eroded by the lack of political will to maintain them.

23

Never too Old

The Mother's Union and Guild was now more important to Ann than ever before. She had been widowed two years previously, but the vicar had been more than good to her, visiting and caring. She felt that she was in his debt and for that reason alone she would go on Sundays to church.

She had managed through the sudden harrowing experience of bereavement, with the minimum of sleeping tablets and no tranquillisers at all. It hadn't been easy returning to worship, but she was greatly helped and encouraged by a member of the congregation who had already gone down that road. Now Ann was making regular visits to the mid-week Women's Meeting, and often wondered what she would do without her church connection, which had now become the only interest in her life. The Reverend Corbett, always noted for his pastoral attention, had asked her to think on and learn two verses of the bible, which she acknowledged helped her through her time of vexation and depression.

"For I am persuaded, that neither death, nor life, nor angels, nor principalities, nor powers, nor things present, nor things to come, nor height, nor depth, nor any other creature shall be able to separate us from the love of God which is in Christ Jesus our Lord".

A religious necessity had become a social desir-
ability. Ann wasn't prepared however for the new
emotional experience ahead of her when she agreed to
participate in the committee set up to start mid-week
indoor recreational activities.

She knew the vicar had proposed her for nomina-
tion, and she was duly elected, with little formality. All
members of the committee were known to her although
not on familiar speaking terms. Several weeks passed
and at the end of one sub-committee meeting, she was
kindly run home by Robert Adgey in his Ford car. She
was taking driving lessons, being advised that having
her own transport would not only make her indepen-
dent, but open up the world to her.

She never did relish being dependent on people, or
being confined to her house due to lack of mobility.
Robert Adgey was a widower of five years standing, a
good churchman in his day, and even now, as he was
approaching early retirement, never missed Sunday
worship. Ann had always held him in high regard. He
appeared quiet and assured. So it came as a surprise
when he talked freely about himself. He told her many
things, so that he no longer was the detached acquaintance. Yes, he never missed a Sunday at church, but it
was really more a matter of strict self-discipline.
Robert confessed that he drove himself to do certain
things: the Sunday morning service gave him a reason
for getting up and getting out of the house. He didn't
care what hymns they sang, what prayers they said or
even what the sermon was about. Ann was disarmed
completely by Robert's honesty. She found herself
slightly attracted to him because he was so candid. She
thought that, when you reach that age, you probably
shut up like a clam and become an introvert, or don't
give twopence what you say and when, provided you

get an audience. Ann was eight years younger than Robert.

She could understand that his health just might not be as perfect as he would wish. She herself had her 'ups and downs' and would have to see her doctor soon. An operation was probable, but she didn't breathe a word of this to a soul. There wasn't anyone she could tell. She had no one. Ann reflected on how alone she was. It wasn't a healthy thought, and she had dwelt on it many times during the last year.

She felt flattered that Robert Adgey should have spoken in such personal terms, but she was determined to be more circumspect. The trouble was that each, in his or her own way, was lonely and just being able to talk freely to someone who had no family ties was in itself a comfort. She thought that when she passed her driving test and purchased her new car then she would have her independence and wouldn't have to rely on anyone for transport. None the less, she found herself looking forward to Sunday.

If she were asked, she would have to admit that she went to church on Sunday hoping to see if Robert Adgey was there for a friendly talk – nothing more; although a woman instinctively knows when a man has an interest in her.

The telephone rang in Vicar Corbett's study. "62910. This is the Manse – Vicar Corbett."

A vaguely disturbed feminine voice replied, "I'm one of your members, and I just want to tell you that two of your committee are possibly misbehaving. Mr Adgey and Mrs Ann Gould have been seen in very unusual places especially after church meetings. It's so indecent after her bereavement. I thought I'd let you know. What do you think about that?"

The Revd Corbett didn't wish to admit it, but he

knew there might be one or two people who attended church just to chat, exchange news and run over personal stories, hoping to hear of a scandal. That someone, whom they judged as undesirable, might be present at worship that day and this would give them endless joy in gossiping for the rest of the week.

But worse was the anonymous letter and telephone call which maligned the good name of any of his regular flock with innuendo.

Vicar Corbett quickly steadied himself, "I'm absolutely delighted that Mr Adgey and Mrs Gould have become friends. I sincerely hope that something good and permanent results. You can be sure I have their happiness at heart – Good-night!"

He stood ruminating in an angry way and telling himself that he should have rebuked the woman by quoting 'Honi soit qui mal y pense' but then would she have understood that.

Slowly he realised that he was glad he hadn't been pedantic and uncharitable. Perhaps a quote from Scripture would have been more appropriate. He saw the irony that he himself was never too old – too old to learn.

24

Join the Club

Being a Christian means being a member of an international club – the greatest and best in the world.

I only realised that when I accepted new employment away from home. It was only natural that I should
go and worship on the first Sunday in a church that
approximated most closely to my own denomination,
and I was fortunate to find a place with which I could
identify in some respects.

It made it easier because, apart from the mutual trust
and warmth, there were other things in common on
which I and my new Christian friends discoursed. I
found this even more so when subsequently I left
Britain to go to Africa and, later, America. No matter in
what culture, or in whatever part of the world you find
yourself, the same Christian love, welcome and acceptance manifests itself, whether it be at a Baptist service
or at Roman Catholic chapel prayers.

Of course, it is preferable to commune with your
own creed, but not, in the eyes of God necessary. How
much more can we learn, how richer our lives, how
deeper our spirituality, how better our Christianity,
when we get out of our little corners and meet and mix
with other believers, other denominations! Some
would say we should not take that risk. Where is the
risk if you are in a strange town in a strange country,

and you know the only people to help you are from some Christian group?

Is it wrong to go out purposely and seek their help, solicit their kindness, play on their tolerance and generosity? We know true Christians will help each other in mutual and reciprocal trust and love. Isn't that what it is all about?

Some could accuse my wife and I of being sycophantic, sponging on the goodness of other Christians. We know that is only too easy – since there are many kind people – also a few gullible ones, but is it wrong to go to church with the purpose of getting help from other believers? This is a strange town for us, but we'll join a church and obtain help. I am a joiner by trade and have plans to build my own house. What I'd like to do is simply to form a group of four or five so-minded Christians, who may have other skills and expertise. Together, by mutual help and pooling individual skills and finances, we would all have our houses built for a fraction of the cost that would have been incurred should we have requested single individual tenders in the open market.

I know the wonderful experience it can be working in a *To-day* situation with fellow believers. The same group of people could easily turn their attention to the fabric of the church building as many items of disrepair can be renewed, or made good, with voluntary labour. One is reminded of a missionary in a novel who converted a number of Indians in South America and helped them, purely by providing daily sustenance.

Their new God was good to them. However when the food was in short supply, their faith evaporated quickly and the poor priest wondered where he had gone wrong as very few then attended his chapel.

It's not like that with us. Our faith doesn't depend on

receiving help from anyone; but our faith expects help from everyone.

Not long after we were converted, our pastor took us into his confidence. He said his formula was to make people laugh. If you can make them laugh, you can make them cry. If you can make them cry, then you had them. You had them for Christ.

It may sound reprehensible to some, but sometimes the end justifies the means. So it is with our convictions of mutual assistance.

There's a friend of mine, who looks after his aged father, who at the age of eighty is confined to the house and spends most of his time in his bed. This friend is locked into a situation which sees no end.

Imagine arising in the morning and looking after the basic needs of an old man before you go to your work, where your mind continually casts back to the problem. Then at five o'clock returning home to the same problem with *all* the domestic chores thrown in. "Tomorrow, and tomorrow, and tomorrow . . . "

Would that not depress you – with little help provided by the social services? Would that not make you weary and worried, bitter, anxious, discouraged? That man came to us and asked us bluntly for help. He needed relief and openly solicited assistance. He said he was due it from other Christians, as he always attended worship when he could.

We present ourselves at the House of God to worship. Some of us may be empty vessels, others running over.

We are there to ask of each other to respond, to give and to receive.

Some may be fully paid up members – others only adherents.

25

The Great Occasions

Any majestic regal, State or Church event in St. Paul's Cathedral or Westminster Abbey, when seen on television, fills me with awe, wonder and reverence. My own church, however, like most, is at the other end of the scale, being a humble, unpretentious, non-conformist building of no architectural virtue.

Despite the poor condition of the paintwork on its walls, despite the deficiency of an acceptable heating standard, despite the drabness of its furniture, despite all that, and the absence of other desirable items, I attend every Sunday morning service. It is then, and only then, I feel and know I belong to the family of God. To know that, all over the country and even the world, though not at the precise same time, on that day, there is universal Christian worship is an encouragement and reassurance.

Then in addition, there are important dates which mean so much – Easter – Whitsun – Christmas – when once again I know that I am participating in a world-wide event of significant importance.

As Christians we are tied to great historical traditions of the past. Those sects that have no tradition must surely labour and struggle and must certainly be the poorer for such an omission. Easter, the great festival to commemorate the resurrection, is celebrated everywhere. The English tradition falls far short of the Eastern Orthodox and the Roman Catholics, who, on the continent especially, have great pageantry with grand candlelight processions on Easter Eve, displaying their crucifixes and ikons of sacred personages.

Who could fail to be moved by such symbolism which helps to focus people's faith and understanding? Then there are the great dramatic performances, the choral works, the dances, the plays, the songs, all reinforcing the faith, when again music is a universal language that transcends individual doctrines and beliefs.

I marvel at these special universal events in the Christian calendar, where there is a mixture of solemnity and jubilation.

I discover the big occasion helps me to think big, about life and God.

Then Christmas with the Nativity story has its own special message. Perhaps I am fortunate in being able to have achieved this attitude of being personally involved and being part of this great celebration, but it hasn't been without meditation. I believe it is a gift from God for us all.

Then again, the great State, Parliamentary or Monarchical pageants involving clerical participation, when listened to or seen on the media, mean much more to me because of my Christian faith.

A Royal Wedding, with the religious ceremonial and sacred music, underpins the Nation's faith. The grandeur and majesty of such an event must lift the Nation's spirits as it does mine.

The rich regalia gracing the occasion, and the traditional Anglican liturgy solemnifies and endorses the importance of the moment.

In all these great affairs – the imagery, symbolism and ceremonial help to explain abstract values in tangible ways, to express spiritual dimensions in natural form and human words.

Al these glorious Church occasions help me to rededicate myself – they provide an act of consecration.

But magnificent as these State events are, equally great are the special religious happenings in my own church. The holy sacraments of marriage and baptism are occasions for joy, tempered with humility and reverence, and can have a real lasting impact for good on the guests and onlookers in the congregation, quite apart from personal meaningful ritual to the participants.

I defy anyone to be present at a solemnization of matrimony ceremony without being moved in a religious sense, albeit only fleeting and temporary. Marriage is a holy estate, and a wedding indeed a great occasion, which everyone wills it to be.

The great occasions are only so because men and women throughout history have desired to recognise God as being in the midst of their eventful lives. They are only as meaningful as people want to make them, but remain opportunities for worship.

Unexpectedly, going to church can result in a rewarding defining moment, a rekindling of the human spirit, a new beginning – indeed a great occasion.